AC

...OOK

By Caroline Bentley-Davies

Published by:

Teachers' Pocketbooks
Laurel House, Station Approach,
Alresford, Hampshire SO24 9JH, UK
Tel: +44 (0)1962 735573
Fax: +44 (0)1962 733637
Email: sales@teacherspocketbooks.co.uk
Website: www.teacherspocketbooks.co.uk

*Teachers' Pocketbooks is an imprint of
Management Pocketbooks Ltd.*

Series editor – Linda Edge

This edition published 2015.
ISBN 978 1 906610 81 4

E-Book ISBN 978 1 908284 66 2

British Library Cataloguing-in-Publication Data
– A catalogue record for this book is available
from the British Library.

Design, typesetting and graphics by efex Ltd.
Printed in U.K.

Contents

Foreword

Broadly speaking, if you were educated before the mid-1990's it's unlikely that your teachers would have been hearing and using the phrase 'raising achievement' anything like as often as teachers today. Although schools hoped that you would fulfil your potential – it didn't always happen.

Times have changed. We now have a wealth of internal and external data to track pupils' achievement and we know from this that some groups of pupils often underachieve. These days, schools and teachers are expected to find strategies to 'close the gap', to make sure *all* pupils maximise their opportunities for success. There are various resources to help with this.

The *Raising Achievement Pocketbook* is for everyone in schools who is involved in helping pupils achieve, whether you are new to teaching, a teaching assistant or an experienced senior leader. It will give you plenty of practical ideas for maximising achievement, some models of good practice, and strategies for leading improvements. It will share research findings on how pupils make progress and, importantly, provide workable suggestions and guidance for applying these to raise results within your classroom and across your school.

Myths and Reality

Why raising achievement matters

There are many reasons why raising achievement amongst our students matters:

- The moral imperative to ensure that every child achieves the best they can at school
- Research shows that pupils who reach their full potential at school have better life prospects. Achievement at school affects future success
- Ensuring equality of opportunity: schools that are effective at raising achievement ensure that all pupils succeed regardless of their gender, race or background
- Improving society. Schools that are successful in raising achievement in their area can break a culture of low aspiration and re-energise the local community
- Your personal success (and pay!) as a teacher will be largely determined by how well your pupils achieve

My sons' teachers know in detail how they are doing. They act quickly if things aren't going so well, and the boys get so much support. As parents we're involved in their learning and we know what we can do to help. If only I'd received that sort of support at school... ...
(Andrew, a pupil in the 1980's)

Eight common myths

Before we look in detail at how we can raise achievement, it's worth exploding some commonly held myths.

Myth 1

The answer is always to do more!

In some schools there's a sense that teachers should be doing more than ever before. Of course, there's a place for some groups of pupils to receive extra tuition (for a limited amount of time), but a never-ending programme of extra classes is unsustainable and research shows that its effectiveness fades over time.

Reality:

If you find that you are always needing to run 'catch up' classes then review how effectively your class is taught the topic in the first place. Pupils don't always make the best of learning opportunities in lessons – especially if they know that the material will always be revisited in extra lessons.

Myth 2

Taking a scatter gun approach

The idea that a strategy or intervention will raise results is very seductive. Before you know it, you have agreed to try out five new, different teaching schemes, signed up for lunch-time classes and have started up every new initiative going. This can lead to you becoming so busy that your essential marking and lesson planning slips.

Reality:

Focus on the areas of underachievement that are most critical to your students' success. Doing something thoroughly will have more impact on achievement than undertaking dozens of 'interventions' in a half-hearted way.

Myth 3

You can't change some pupils' poor attitudes towards learning

Some pupils are easy to motivate – it's a fact! Whatever you tell them to do they'll do it. These pupils meet their targets because they work hard to improve upon their identified weaknesses; however other students just seem impossible to motivate.

Reality:

You can't give someone motivation – but you can create the right climate for it to grow, so that pupils want to succeed, believe they can succeed, and feel supported in reaching their goals. Some teachers can inspire and propel the seemingly impossible student. They use engaging teaching strategies and show their belief that all their pupils can improve. (More on this later in the section, *Metacognition and Motivation*.)

Myth 4

Just switch and win!

There's an easier examination board/ magic writing programme or Maths intervention that will solve all problems.

'The school down the road achieved a 98% pass rate just by changing to the 'easier' examination board or buying a scheme. Let's do that too!'

It is very easy to fall prey to the powers of a good marketing campaign.

Reality:

Everyone likes a quick fix, but improving results is not that simple. If we decide to change, we must fully understand the assessment criteria, new materials and demands of the board. If schools do improve after seemingly 'just switching', it will be because this change is underpinned by a lot of thorough extra preparation, research and focused effective lessons.

Myth 5

Just focus on 'tests-taking' pupils

Raising achievement is all about exam students or those at the end of a Key Stage. These 'key' groups of students receive most extra efforts, resources and intervention programmes because they're the ones whose assessments count in school league tables.

Reality:

It is natural to focus on those who are about to be assessed; however gaps in pupil skills will have started showing a lot earlier in a child's education. If weaknesses aren't addressed in earlier years there will be far too much to 'catch up' in the final years. The Year 11 student who was told after her mock exams that she needed to improve her vocabulary range to attain her target grade realised that this was something she needed to have been focusing on since Year 7 rather than trying to rectify the problem at such a late stage.

Myth 6

It's all my responsibility!

It's disheartening when individual pupils don't make as much progress as they should. You are the class teacher and of course the ultimate responsibility is yours.

Reality:

Other staff and stakeholders should be involved too. You need to alert your middle leaders if there are wider issues that might be leading to underachievement. Persistent pupil absences; poor behaviour across the school; a lack of vital teaching resources; insecure teacher knowledge about the latest examination requirements, these all exacerbate underachievement. We can identify these issues as class teachers, but solving them may well require external assistance, support or funding.

Myth 7

Doing it for them is the best way

We want pupils to succeed so we try to make everything as easy as possible for them. We supply revision notes for them. If they can't be bothered to bring equipment we provide it. We don't really make them think for themselves because we need to help them pass – at any cost!

Reality:

Doing everything for pupils, 'spoon feeding' them, is counterproductive. Pupils become complacent and over-reliant on their teachers. They don't try to work things out for themselves, write their own notes or grapple with learning. This makes them less independent and unable to think for themselves in projects, tests – and in life.

Myth 8

More able pupils don't really underachieve

When asked to think of underachieving pupils, we don't tend to think of our more able pupils. Most of them achieve results that are better than the national average – so can they really be underachieving?

Reality:

Any pupils failing to reach their full potential are underachieving. There's a huge issue with underachieving 'high ability' pupils. Ofsted highlighted this using data from over 2,000 lesson observations finding that:

- *Only in a fifth of lessons were the 'more able' supported well or better... and*
- *In 40% of the schools visited the more able students were not making the progress of which they were capable.*

(The Most Able Students, Ofsted June 2013)

What Raising Achievement Looks Like

In a nutshell

Here's what successful schools focus on in raising achievement:

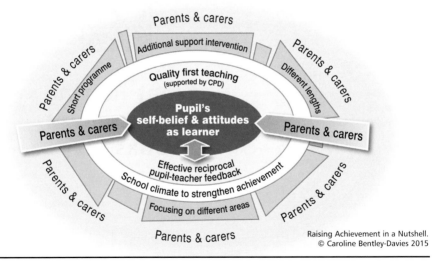

Raising Achievement in a Nutshell.
© Caroline Bentley-Davies 2015

In a nutshell

Notice how the pupil is at the centre of their learning. Pupils only take on advice and make good progress if they see themselves as effective learners. Their attitudes towards learning are bolstered when the **school's climate of achievement** reinforces high standards and champions improvements.

Quality first teaching and **effective reciprocal feedback** appear in the second circle. These are the two most influential ways teachers can help students to maximize their achievement. (Schools that invest in staff **CPD** invest wisely. Their teachers are more likely to deliver consistently good lessons leading to a rise in results.)

Some pupils will need learning support or social/ emotional/ behavioural support. Such interventions will be regularly reviewed and may be temporary or ongoing; the diagram represents these '**additional interventions**' in segments.

Parents and carers appear all around the circle since their influence lies mainly outside of school but of course can affect all areas. However, they are also shown across the core, as schools increasingly work to engage parents/ carers with multiple aspects of raising achievement.

Who is involved in raising achievement?

1. Class teacher

The most essential person in motivating pupils and tracking their progress is the class teacher. Successful teachers know their pupils inside out. This means making use of previous data about your students to ensure that you:

- Know their current attainment and past progress
- Understand their potential and, therefore, what their target should be
- Know their strengths and weaknesses in particular areas
- Know them as individuals to learn how to motivate them
- Adapt lessons and materials to challenge and engage all pupils
- Are aware of key issues that might affect their progress, eg absence, home circumstances, specific special educational needs

Be aware of any funding you could access to support your students' learning.

Who is involved in raising achievement?

2. Teaching assistant

Underachieving pupils are often allocated time with a teaching assistant. This might be within a lesson or as part of a targeted programme to increase their skills in a specific area, such as phonics or Maths. To make sure that pupils make good progress there needs to be:

- Good initial liaison with the class teacher so that the intervention is based on pupils' real needs
- An approach that develops their independence and ability to think for themselves
- Tracking and assessing of progress so that the intervention can be adapted and monitored
- Feedback to the class teacher so that lessons build on the pupils' current learning

Who is involved in raising achievement?

3. Senior/ middle leaders
Successful schools have leadership teams who are effective in closing achievement gaps.

They understand that improving achievement is a process, not just a list of things to do.

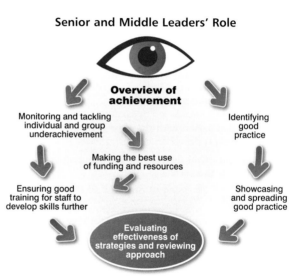

Senior and Middle Leaders' Role

Overview of achievement

Monitoring and tackling individual and group underachievement

Identifying good practice

Making the best use of funding and resources

Ensuring good training for staff to develop skills further

Showcasing and spreading good practice

Evaluating effectiveness of strategies and reviewing approach

One size doesn't fit all

How exactly you raise achievement will depend on the reason for the lack of good progress and the needs of the pupil. One size doesn't fit all! Look at the following three examples of underachieving students and how differently their situations were tackled.

1. Extra subject support

Alex is a very shy pupil in Year 4. He excels in several subjects but struggles in Maths. He is in a large class where he sits next to an able friend, whose work he appears to be copying. Any extra Maths Alex is given for homework is 'lost'. He is falling behind in his learning.

Action: Alex is moved to sit with a pupil of similar ability. 'Talking time' is promoted so pupils can discuss solutions to problems. His teacher sees that Alex has several conceptual misunderstandings about Mathematics. He receives a six-week series of extra 'catch up' lessons, involving one-to-one support with a teaching assistant. He joins a Maths booster club with online resources and his parents are contacted to discuss how to encourage him to use it at home.

One size doesn't fit all

2. Resources, emotional support and space to study

In some situations a student might have the academic skills to improve their achievement, but lack the resources or emotional support needed for success.

Shannon doesn't have a quiet space to study. She has five siblings and her home is classed as overcrowded. She has no IT, books, equipment or emotional support available to help with homework. She is underachieving as she doesn't have the resources needed to improve her work.

Intervention: GCSE study rooms for use at lunch and after school are set up. These provide resources, including IT and snacks as well as 'Sixth Form Subject Specialists' on hand to help. Shannon's form tutor liaises with her teachers to ensure that school-funded equipment is provided for all courses, including the loan of a laptop. She is also supported as part of the school's academic mentoring system.

One size doesn't fit all

3. Teacher support

Sometimes groups or large numbers of pupils in one class are underachieving.

In one Y9 Science class the majority of pupils are underachieving. They have a poor work ethic and do not bother completing homework or trying in class. The class teacher feels inexperienced in the subject and has got the class using textbooks most of the time to control their behaviour.

Intervention: The teacher 'buddied up' with a colleague who had a parallel set and shared resources and successful teaching ideas. She now uses the school policy to deal with behaviour issues and ensures that missing homework is followed up. Behaviour management training and some specific Science KS3 training have helped her make lessons more effective and engaging.

From doing to reviewing

When it comes to raising achievement, deciding what to do and doing it are just the first steps. You need to continuously review, reflect and adapt what you are doing to ensure it is successful. So, before you start:

- Who exactly is underachieving?
- What are the specific issues?
- What do you want to achieve?
- What resources, time or money, or support will it take?
- How will you review it?
- How will you measure whether it has been effective or not?
- How will you flex and adapt what you have learnt?

The big dipper!

Bear in mind that pupils' performance often dips between Key Stages, when they move class or transfer from primary to secondary or from infant to junior school. It is a good idea for pupils to forward examples of their 'best work', reading records etc. to their new teachers so that they don't accept inferior work, mistakenly thinking it is the best a pupil can do.

Make sure you also:

- Talk to the previous class teacher about which teaching strategies have been successful
- Moderate work between teachers and classes so that there is a common agreement, for instance, about what a grade A looks like at 'A Level'
- Talk to the pupil about where they have succeeded in the past and what strategies worked for them
- Are aware of, and discuss with parents and carers, any issues that might be adversely influencing a pupil's learning

Finding good practice

Dealing with underachievement can seem a daunting task. We need to know where to find good practice to answer the key question: *'How can I improve my pupils' rates of progress?'* Research from OECD found that: *variation in performance* **within** *individual schools is four times greater than variation across schools.*

So before racing off to find out what other schools are doing, it is worth locating good practice within your own school first. Finding out which subjects or teachers are making the most progress with their pupils and then finding out exactly how they do this is a good first step.

The kinds of strategies these teachers are likely to be using will include delivering powerful feedback, using engaging teaching techniques, developing an effective learning climate, encouraging growth mindsets and metacognition, etc, all things we'll be looking at later in this book.

Climate for Achievement

Creating a 'can do' culture

We've seen how various targeted interventions can boost achievement but raising achievement is not just about 'add ons' for small groups or individuals. Research indicates that the most effective strategies for raising pupil achievement include learning approaches and attitudes that *all* teachers should be undertaking with *all* their pupils.

This section of the Pocketbook looks at how to create a climate for developing better achievement within lessons and more widely within the school culture.

Let's start with a look at the diagram that follows. For each section of the wheel note down your strengths or things you do to be successful in this area. Assign yourself a mark from 1-5, where 5 is 'highly effective' and 1 indicates you could do with some extra ideas. Join the marks up on the wheel to help you think about where you are and where you need to get to.

Creating a 'can do' culture

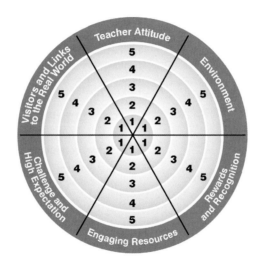

'Can Do' Culture Wheel. © Caroline Bentley-Davies 2015

Teachers set the weather!

In our classrooms we are in charge of the weather. We set it by our behaviour.

Setting the tone for a good learning climate in your classroom is crucial for pupils to achieve their full potential. You have to make pupils believe that they can achieve and you can do this in various ways:

- Using positive language
- Using body language that reinforces the positive comments
- Following through on your promises and remembering homework set, etc
- Encouraging pupils to try for themselves and building learning resilience
- Presenting yourself as a learner and modelling learning behaviours

Great expectations

A pupil's self-belief is a reflection of their teacher's attitudes. If a teacher doesn't believe their students can master a difficult topic, their students certainly won't believe they can.

True story

An examiner running GCSE revision classes in a school was told she would meet a class of high flying pupils, and a class of weaker students with poor attitudes and behaviour. Assuming the first group were the high flyers, she began by telling them she expected great things from them and how their teacher had praised them. She set them a tough challenge, which they attacked determinedly. When their initial answers fell short, she pressed and encouraged them to develop their ideas. They rose to the task with excellent results.

At the end of the lesson, the class teacher rushed over saying she had never seen the 'bottom set' work so hard!

Pupils rise or fall to our expectations; we need to set those expectations high!

Underachieving groups and school climate

In some schools specific groups of students underachieve. The exact make-up of these will vary from school to school. A thorough exploration of your school's RAISEonline report will highlight any underachieving groups.

We need to ensure that barriers facing **any** pupils are overcome and that **everyone** wants to achieve. In some schools the ethos is that it is 'cool' to succeed; in others class teachers strive to develop their own 'micro climate' of achievement within their lessons. What can we do to foster this important 'can do' climate in all lessons?

Four steps to improving climate for achievement

1 Believe that all pupils can achieve.

2 Use positive, directive comments.

3 Set challenging tasks.

4 Encourage accurate self-reflection.

Step 1 – Believe that all pupils can achieve

Teachers who are skilled in raising achievement know they must be credible with their students. Just telling them that they will pass their exam is not good enough. The best teachers know the target achievements of their pupils and know what to expect from them. They always aim high!

Share your belief that your students will pass – but ground it in concrete actions. Wishful thinking never passed any examinations.

Formula for success

Belief that pupils have the aptitude to succeed +

Positive directive comments +

Challenging tasks +

Accurate pupil self-reflection

= Academic
   success

Step 2 – Positive directive comments

Great teachers enthuse, inspire and motivate pupils. The words you say can make pupils want to give the lesson their best shot. Using language effectively can both motivate and empower your students:

Great teachers don't say:	Because the pupil hears:	Instead, raising achievement comment	Effect on pupil
You will get a grade 8.	*Great I don't need to do anything.*	You've got the potential to get a grade 8. You need to do x …	*Sir believes I can do it – but there are specific things I must do. I'd better do them.*
This is really easy…	*I don't have to put any effort in (what's the point?). Or if they can't do it: I must be stupid – she's said it's easy!*	This is challenging, but I know you are ready for it. You will make mistakes –that's fine you are learning.	Understands that learning can be hard but that progress will be made. Mistakes are part of learning.
Hand your work in. I will mark it.	*I don't need to check it because Miss will correct it for me.*	Before you hand your work in highlight where you have included all of the success criteria.	*I'd better look over my work and check I've included all of the necessary details.*

Step 3 – Challenging tasks

Research compiled by John Hattie in his book *Visible Learning* shows that one of the reasons pupils fail to achieve is that the tasks they are given are not sufficiently challenging to push them into realms of new learning.

For pupils to reach their potential we need to encourage them to aim beyond their comfort zone. If pupils are aiming for a grade C and they are working at the C/D border, showing them exemplar C grade work often won't help. The grade C work shares too many characteristics with their current work. However, showing them an example of grade B work and highlighting what it achieves that their work doesn't, helps them more readily see the steps they need to make to progress.

Try saying:

> *Although this piece of work is several grades higher than your target grade, you can see how it includes the kind of effective examples you could use to improve the quality of your work.*

Step 3 – Challenging tasks

In your quest to raise achievement, you will need to take some bold steps to create an appetite for challenge. Three things to remember:

- A key reason pupils improve is that they are being pushed to experiment with new ways of thinking. Encourage students to think for themselves and to develop mastery of the subject
- The challenging task, while it may stretch your students, must be achievable
- Make time in lessons to consolidate and review learning. When challenge is too low, bored students switch off and don't learn; equally, constant high challenge without support can also lead to low achievement

The key to success is encouraging pupils to see failure as part of the learning process. My students regularly get things wrong and that's okay – they ultimately learn better because of this constant challenge. **(Teacher with regularly exceptional results)**

Step 4: Accurate pupil self-reflection

Lessons where pupils are regularly encouraged to reflect on their learning and their strategies for learning secure better results. Students who are able to accurately self-assess (commenting on their strengths and weaknesses of their work) make the most progress. These are complex skills to teach, but the ability to self-reflect isn't just a skill for older students to master. Even the youngest pupils can make huge strides with this; it needs to be part of the learning climate.

This example from an infant school shows how teachers foster self–reflection within a lesson:

They had a common approach to reviewing lessons. Lessons had regular 'learning stops'. Pupils talked fluently about what they had achieved and what they did not fully understand.

(Ofsted report on Assessment for Learning.)

Looks matter

We might be fostering a climate of achievement in our actions and attitudes as teachers, but the physical environment can help too. We give away our expectations of pupils before we even start our lesson. Look at these descriptions of two school's classrooms. They speak for themselves:

School A: The classroom walls are bare, except for a formal message board. This is because some of the work was not of good enough quality to display. There is a tracking system showing pupils' assessments on the wall. Most are colour coded red (showing insufficient progress).

School B: Walls show high quality pupil work with attached teacher explanations. Key vocabulary connected to the current topics is displayed. There is a reward board and displays of 'Work of the Week'. There is further information about learning resources, QR codes and websites for pupils to access to support self-study.

Displays that foster achievement and involvement

The best displays engage pupils, highlight achievements and further learning, eg:

Showcase future careers of recent successful ex-pupils. Include photograph of the pupil, information about their career, why they enjoy it, and explain why studying that subject helped them succeed.

Review it. National Literacy Trust www.literacytrust.org.uk research indicates the best way to promote reading is by personal recommendation. A primary school has a colourful reading tree. Pupils fill out a 'leaf' reviewing a book they have enjoyed reading, so inspiring others.

Real world relevance. Display newspaper articles and job advertisements, labelled to show how your subject is relevant to everyday life. For example, in a Maths classroom, displaying 'jobs in this area' with annotations showing how mathematical knowledge is needed for a range of posts can be quite a motivator.

Displays that foster achievement and involvement

Question Wall. When they start a topic, pupils come up with questions they would like answered. These are placed on the wall. Periodically, the teacher reviews the questions with pupils to see if any answers have been found. Pupils add answers and move the questions along the board when they have answered them. Progress in action!

Beat the Teacher! The teacher phrases a weekly challenge question that demands some working out and detail from pupils. Pupils place their answers in the envelope pockets displayed on the board. There is a prize for the winner.

Challenge envelopes are stuck on the wall containing 'challenges' connected to the current topic. Pupils can select an extra challenge, for instance to make their story writing more demanding, perhaps by writing from the perspective of an object, by including different 'flash backs', or by writing in a similar style to the extract from a famous novel. Envelopes are colour-coded to show the level of demand.

Displays for success

Displays that show pupils how to succeed make achievement seem realistic.

Level up!
One History teacher uses a display to show how pupils can 'level up' and improve their work. Examples of work at different stages are enlarged and photocopied. These are annotated with large arrows highlighting what has been achieved and what would make the work even better. Pupils find the display invaluable as it shows them exactly what they need to do to improve their work, as they can see work at a range of different levels.

Taking it further
One teacher created the concept of a visual ladder running up the wall. When pupils respond to a question, if she feels that they could add more or improve their work she asks them to 'move up the ladder'. She indicates the improvement in their verbal response by signalling the rung of the ladder they are on. This is a clear way of encouraging students to develop and extend each other's ideas.

Resources

Displays and teacher attitudes are crucial but it is important to have plenty of 'hands on' resources to foster independent learning. Ultimately, unless students can think for themselves, their achievement will be limited.

One primary teacher found that setting up a Maths equipment area in her classroom led pupils to think more deeply about number problems. With easy access to number squares, number lines, counters, bead strings, maths vocab mat, etc and freedom to choose the equipment they thought would help them solve problems, the children moved up a gear in thinking about what they were learning.

Tables with *'Learning Boxes'* can be created for other subject areas. A dictionary, thesaurus and other reading material and articles related to the topic mean that pupils can take steps to check things for themselves and progress their own learning.

Inspirational visitors and experts

Pupils love meeting real-life experts or people who have striven to overcome barriers to success. Such meetings can be inspiring and motivating. Hearing from the experts exactly how to become an athlete, doctor or artist is a concrete way of developing 'learning ambition'. Advice is likely to include: **developing resilience**, **working hard** and the importance of **regular practice**.

Arranging visits linked to specific subjects can also inspire students. Organisations like the National Association of Writers in Education www.nawe.co.uk have an online directory of writers who run workshops to inspire pupils. Likewise, subject associations are good places to find information about visitors connected with your subject area.

Often parents and ex pupils have interesting careers that can trigger an idea or interest. Speakers for Schools www.speakers4schools.org provides leading speakers to state schools free of charge.

www.inspiringthefuture.org is another free service linking state schools/ colleges with speakers from all professions who are prepared to talk about their careers.

Rewards and recognition

Pupils are motivated when their hard work is recognised and rewarded, eg by being displayed in public, published in the school newsletter, shown to the class or highlighted to the Head. Equally, contacting home when pupils have done well can transform occasional effort into a long-term improvement in attitude.

A great classroom climate encourages pupils to want to learn and try hard without external motivators. However, you can boost student motivation by **catching them working hard** and by giving them **specific feedback**:

> *Well done, Tariq, you labelled the diagram thoughtfully and accurately. Now can you explain the solution by writing three more sentences that include the key words?*

In lessons where pupils don't want to learn, positive comments are often thin on the ground. Research (eg Trussell, 2008) shows that increasing the number of positive comments to negative to 4:1 has a constructive effect on student learning and behaviour. Other researchers suggest an even higher ratio. Try it – it really works!

The next chapter will explore in more detail how feedback can raise achievement.

Feedback Matters

Research evidence

There's a wealth of academic research evidencing ways to improve pupils' achievement. The Sutton Trust research data and John Hattie's synthesis of raising achievement research are two examples I'll be referring to regularly. Both highlight the importance of feedback.

1. Sutton Trust – Education Endowment Foundation Research

The Teaching and Learning Toolkit was originally commissioned in 2011 by the Sutton Trust whose aim is to 'improve social mobility through education'. The research is a compilation of the different strategies and interventions schools might spend money on to raise pupil achievement, each summarised in terms of their average impact on attainment, the strength of the evidence and their cost.

Schools have been encouraged to use the Toolkit to decide how best to spend 'Pupil Premium' funding, awarded for groups of students that are typically at risk of underachievement. The research is empowering in that it highlights the most effective things that *all* teachers can do to raise achievement in *all* of their classes, regardless of their pupils' backgrounds. The Toolkit is now a live resource, updated as new research becomes available www.suttontrust.com

Sutton Trust – Educational Endowment Foundation research

The table below shows some of the top, proven strategies for raising achievement that feature in the Toolkit. They are categorised to show best value for money, as well as reliability of the research evidence.

Approach	Cost	Reliability of evidence summary	Impact estimate
Feedback	££	***	+ 8 months
Metacognition and self-regulation	££	****	+ 8 months
Peer tutoring	££	****	+ 6 months
Reading comprehension strategies	£	****	+ 5 months
Collaborative learning	£	****	+ 5 months

Average impact is estimated in terms of the additional months of progress you might expect pupils to make as a result of an approach being used in school, taking average pupil progress over a year as a bench mark.

(*The Sutton Trust-EEF Teaching and Learning Toolkit*, April 2015)

Research evidence

2. Visible learning – John Hattie

In his book *Visible Learning* John Hattie presents *'a synthesis of over 800 meta-analyses relating to achievement'*. He shows how his compilation of research might be applied in the classroom to raise student achievement by indicating the 'effect size' for each possible teaching approach or strategy listed.

The calculation of effect size is complicated, but – simplified – an effect size of 0.40 is the point at which we can notice an appreciable impact on student achievement. Interventions between 0.50 and 1.2 are said to have a **high effect** and are in the 'zone of desired effects'. Both feedback, with a 0.75 effect size, and metacognitive strategies (see next chapter) at 0.69 feature as highly effective here and in the Sutton Trust findings. Currently top of Hattie's list is self-reported grades, while surprisingly low effects are seen for homework.

Research for school-wide improvements

Research figures and statistics are thought-provoking and it is wise to learn from the successes of others. However, schools, classes and individuals all have different contexts and needs. Best practice from research is an interesting starting point, but we need to be careful to respond to the specific needs and contexts of our individual pupils rather than just changing things as a knee jerk reaction to the latest research.

However much we exercise caution, we can't ignore a potential progress leap of eight months attributed to giving effective feedback to our students. It's one of the most powerful strategies in a teacher's toolkit.

We need to be sure that the feedback we give is clear, precise and useful. It needs to be positive and to signpost the way forward. It should be given promptly, require action on behalf of the pupils and should lead to input from them which can be used to plan subsequent lessons. Read on!

Is feedback clear, precise and useful?

Some schools have multiple methods of scoring pupils' work. Students might receive up to eight different variations and marks from different teachers, which can be really confusing. The research on feedback shows that it is the written **comment** that helps pupils improve, not the **alpha or numeric mark**. But students always look for the mark or grade first. They are either so happy or deflated by it they often don't go on to the really helpful comment.

Tip: Withhold the grade when you first return marked work. Give a comment – and return the score the following lesson. This way students read and engage with the feedback. (Some teachers even write their final comment sideways on the page, building in a visual check that pupils are turning the books to read them.)

Check feedback is understood

Do pupils really understand the comments they receive? Clarity in teaching and in feedback are cited as top factors in raising achievement by several researchers (0.75 effect size according to Hattie).

To test out whether your feedback is useful:

- Have regular one-to-one discussions with pupils. Ask them to talk about their work and the comments you have made. Can they read them? Do they understand them?

- Give out a sticky note at the start of the lesson. Ask pupils to jot down their top areas of improvement. Later compare this to the comments in their books. Is it the same?

- When giving verbal feedback ask pupils to jot down the main points raised – check they accord with what you said

Great feedback has clear focus

2 P's and 2 T's

Good feedback is more than just a pat on the back. To drive improvements it needs to be:

P Positive **T** Thought-provoking

P Precise **T** Tackled by pupils

2 P's

Positive – Students are much more likely do something with your feedback if it is phrased constructively, eg *'Ben your explanation of the after-effects of the earthquake is strong. You included good detail when you discussed the effect on sanitation'.*

Precise – Be crystal clear about what is effective and specific about what could be better. This often means focusing on one area, eg:

'You have explained the experiment clearly using effective scientific vocabulary... Highlight where you have used key terms in your conclusion. There are two places where they could be improved.'

Great feedback has clear focus

2 T's

Thought provoking – the feedback comment should make the pupil think about their work. *'I liked the way you used two different sources to justify your ideas. Why did you think the secondary source provided the best argument?'*

Tackled – Good feedback requires action by the pupil. As teachers we often spend lots of time correcting the same errors. Asking a question, giving students a choice of response or getting them to make a specific improvement is crucial for them to really progress.

'Medals and missions' motivate

Motivated pupils work harder. Great teachers know that using positive terminology helps motivate pupils to want to improve and act on feedback.

> Geoff Petty, in his book *Evidence Based Teaching*, likens effective feedback to giving pupils 'medals and missions'. As he explains it, 'medals' are *'information about what exactly was done well'* ie they recognise and celebrate achievement so far. But to secure improvements, pupils also need 'missions': *'This is information about what the student needs to improve, correct, or work on. It is best when it is forward-looking and positive.'*
>
> Petty also reminds us that having clear goals is essential for success: *'the medals and missions need to be given in relation to clear goals, usually best given in advance.'*

Three steps for effective feedback

 1. Make it prompt.

 2. Make it require action.

 3. Use feedback loops to influence the next lessons.

Step 1 – Make it prompt

In some practical subjects much of the feedback is oral. When you are teaching rugby on the field the comments, demonstrations and responses to pupils' actions are immediate. Pupils know straight away what they are doing well and where they need to improve. Teachers intervene with feedback and see progress in action!

In many subjects (including GCSE PE) written work is marked after the learning has taken place. Students need to receive feedback promptly to avoid repeating errors in future.

Help them recall it If you give oral feedback in a lesson where pupils have books/folders ask them to note down the main points. It is important that they can recall what the feedback actually was.

Step 1 – Make it prompt

Pupils often receive feedback on a specific piece of work only after the teacher has marked the completed piece. We need to check out how well pupils are learning by holding quick feedback sessions as the lesson develops. These allow us both to give and receive crucial feedback on the spot.

An Ofsted report on the quality of 'A Level' Science teaching commended the use of mini whiteboards. The observed teacher used these to ensure that *every* pupil answered the question. She could address misconceptions immediately. Likewise, hand-held devices such as clickers, where pupils can select from a range of appropriate answers, give immediate feedback. If you don't have clickers then *Socrative* and *Kahoot* are two free tools that can be used with i-Pads and other electronic devices to generate pupil feedback. Through a 'virtual classroom pupil list' you can track exactly which pupils need further consolidation of their learning.

Step 2 – Require action

Schools that effectively use feedback to make an impact on learning actively involve students across the entire curriculum. Three examples of successful systems and strategies:

A. Film it
In PE, Dance or Drama, classes, working in groups, film each other completing a task. They then use the clips to immediately review performance. Giving specific verbal feedback helps the participating pupils understand how to evaluate their work. Phrasing comments positively and precisely is crucial, eg:

- What went well? **WWW** (specific comments linked to the learning objective)

- Even better if? **EBI** (what alterations or changes would improve things)

Step 2 – Require action

B. Go MAD!

One school introduced a policy of M.A.D. time (Make a Difference!). Pupils know that they are regularly expected to act on feedback. They are given a MAD target such as a comment or question they must answer, eg:

'Now go on to the next level by explaining your overall thoughts in a summary paragraph, highlighting your personal opinion about the proposed plan'.

Since it's a regular event, MAD time has become an effective strategy in raising achievement across different lessons.

Tip: Some teachers play particularly lively pieces of music while pupils are responding to their corrections. The brisk tempo and short time period can help students focus and it becomes part of the regular learning repertoire in that class.

 # Step 2 – Require action

C. Tickled pink

Primary schools often use coloured highlighters when marking work, to indicate parts that 'tickle them pink'! This simple system works well with all ages, the colour coding helping to ensure clear and specific feedback.

The teacher highlights in pink successful aspects of the student's work. In a persuasive writing task, for instance, this might be good use of adjectives or rhetorical devices. The teacher also comments (on the first example), identifying for the pupil exactly what they are doing well, eg: *'great adjective'*.

Likewise, highlighting a small but specific section in green signifies the 'green shoots for improvement' and gives pupils a very focused area to review and rework.

 # Step 2 – Require action

Suggested actions
Vary the kinds of actions you want pupils to take as a result of your feedback. The improvements will only 'stick' in the pupils' minds if they have acted on them. The following are all good ways of engaging students with feedback:

- Posing questions and asking students to answer them
- Asking them to rephrase or rewrite specific areas with a clear improvement
- Giving a spelling correction and asking them to rewrite it five times
- Giving a definition and asking them to write a sentence using it

Experiment
One Geography teacher found that when she wrote her comments alongside the parts of the work that needed improving pupils were more likely to act on them than if the feedback was incorporated in a final comment at the end!

Step 3 – Feedback loops from pupil to teacher

When we think of effective feedback we most frequently think of teachers feeding back to pupils. However, in *Visible Learning* John Hattie shows the importance of reciprocal feedback. We need to know from our pupils about our teaching. If we know what our students find less successful in helping their learning, we can strive to improve.

Some teachers give pupils a sticky note at the end of the lesson – and ask: *'What helped your learning today, and what could I do better next time?'* You could even poll them about a recent topic or unit you have taught, creating a simple survey via *Survey Monkey* or other online tool. Use their input as pointers to improve your teaching and their learning.

Key Point: Use the feedback you receive from pupils, from your marking and from ongoing observations in lessons to alter and adapt your next lessons to meet their needs.

Improving feedback through modelling

One Head of Languages conducted a mini investigation starting with his own classes. He was giving pupils helpful advice, but they weren't reading or acting on it! Using a visualizer (a piece of ICT equipment to display pupil work to the class) he started phrasing his final marking comment as a question. He spent time showing pupils examples of his comments and modelling how they might respond to his questions.

Once the class were trained in responding to the teacher's marking, they were given a green pen to note their corrections. Time was allocated in class for them to act on the teacher's feedback – in green ink. This 'green pen feedback time' made a real difference to the pupils' learning.

Final thoughts on feedback

Effective feedback raises achievement but it requires commitment from teachers, Teaching Assistants and, most importantly, individual pupils who need to act on it to secure improvements.

Schools that have made really exceptional progress in raising achievement have understood the importance of focusing on feedback and developing practical strategies to embed improvements. The Ofsted report of one school that successfully raised achievement reads:

> *'...above all, the persistence of teachers in setting targets with action points to which students responded in detail, have resulted in consistently better than expected progress.'*
>
> Headteacher. (The Burgate School and Sixth Form Centre) Business and Economics Good Practice Report, Ofsted, (Ref: 120200).

Metacognition and Motivation

Thinking and teaching 'know how'

We want the best for our pupils, but ensuring that is challenging. The following factors might be at play if pupils are underachieving in our classes:

- The need to teach the curriculum in a limited time frame which means that pupils cover ground, but don't really embed their understanding
- Relying on what has worked with previous classes, rather than adapting our teaching to the specific needs of current pupils
- Hard-to-motivate pupils who feel that they can't achieve
- Pupils' susceptibility to peer pressure (particularly at secondary age). They don't want to look 'uncool' by appearing to struggle with their learning

This section looks at how you can develop your own and your students' metacognitive skills (skills that enable us to reflect upon our own thinking and learning habits) and how they can improve their attitudes towards learning challenges.

Students' self-belief and mindset

Pupils' attitudes towards their learning and self-belief really matter. Some students think they can succeed without much effort; they over-estimate their likely success. There's evidence that underachieving boys, in particular, often over-estimate how well they will do in tests and exams, believing it will be 'alright on the night'. They aren't motivated to learn good study habits and by the time the exam occurs it is too late to rectify their mistakes.

'Boys tend to over-estimate their academic abilities. Girls generally underestimate and work harder to compensate.' **(Education Scotland Research Summary)**

Often students fear getting things wrong. Helping them to develop resilience by engendering a positive, but realistic, attitude towards their learning and self-belief is crucial in helping them achieve success.

Teachers' self-belief and mindset

Teachers who consistently help pupils make the most progress model what it means to be a learner. They highlight their own learning, including the thinking strategies *they* use to make headway. This shows students the kind of thought processes needed to work out what to do.

> *'I see this is a complicated diagram. We need to learn these difficult words for the exam. One of the ways I learn unfamiliar words is by writing them out several times, but what other strategies can you think of?'*

Great teachers highlight the tricky areas and show that they are learning too:

> *'Now when I am looking at this test paper I can see that Section B has twice the number of marks as Section A and C. So I'm thinking to myself, I must remember to allocate my time accordingly. How much time should I allocate to Section A?'*

Failure is only the first attempt at learning

Successful teachers believe their pupils can make good progress; they realise that mistakes and failure are learning opportunities and only temporary setbacks. Their outlook rubs off on their students.

The term 'growth mindset' was coined by Professor Carol Dweck. Her book *'Mindsets: How You can Fulfil your Potential'* highlights how those who achieve most in life do so because they are willing to learn from their mistakes and to strive to improve their personal performance. Her research is applied to the classroom and, as Dweck herself says, explained 'elegantly and succinctly' in the *Growth Mindset Pocketbook*.

Teacher with a fixed mindset:
'You didn't do very well on your test. I am disappointed in you. You are supposed to be a top set!'

Teacher with a growth mindset
'As a class you didn't score well on this test. You can do better! What were the challenges in completing this test? What can you do to help yourself learn from this test? Do I need to re-teach any areas?'

Growth mindset in action

True story

A science teacher was dismayed by the attitude of his class. When they received test papers back, they only looked at their mark. They felt disillusioned and downcast if they'd scored poorly, and relieved if they'd scored well. No one was interested in learning how to improve.

Determined to get pupils to see that they could learn from and improve their exam scores, the teacher photocopied the papers before marking them and got pupils reviewing the unscored papers of their classmates. He explained the mark scheme, empowering them to see how to gain full marks. He tutored them through the examining process so pupils knew exactly what they needed to do to succeed.

On receiving their marked papers back, students set themselves specific learning targets based on topics or aspects they needed to improve. Although this approach was time-consuming, pupils really 'owned' their corrections and targets. Their scores improved massively next time round.

How do you ensure that pupils 'own' their mistakes and see them as learning opportunities?

Metacognition matters

When teaching examination classes, the amount of material you need to cover can feel overwhelming. It's tempting to take shortcuts, but if you don't engage students in active thinking, their learning is not secure. To get the higher grades, they need to be able to challenge and evaluate ideas, rather than just having a superficial grasp.

> ## True story
>
> An English teacher was working very hard to teach pupils one of the scores of poems needed for the GCSE Literature exam they were sitting in three months' time. She worked up a sweat telling them exactly what they needed to know about a particular poem, passing on her expert knowledge.
>
> The following day her student teacher was due to teach the next poem on the list. However, she started her lesson with a cut-up version of the previous day's poem, asking pupils to quickly sequence it. They couldn't! They had passively experienced the previous lesson without engagement with or understanding the poem.

What interactive teaching strategies have you used recently to really get pupils thinking for themselves?

Quality first teaching

'No amount of additional intervention can compensate for a lack of good quality teaching' **(key message from the 2014 SEN Code of Practice)**

No matter how many any extra 'catch up' sessions, mounds of homework or other 'additional' interventions you provide, it's quality, differentiatied 'first teaching' that is the main foundation for assuring achievement.

It's **what we do in lessons** that really determines the amount of progress pupils make. Both the Sutton Trust and John Hattie's compilation of research identify **metacognition** and **pupil self-regulation strategies*** as being responsible for helping pupils make up to eight months' worth of additional progress. This is huge, so let's see what these strategies might look like in everyday classroom practice.

* Metacognition 'is sometimes known as 'learning to learn' and 'self-regulation strategies' means managing one's own motivations towards learning. The intention is to give pupils a repertoire of strategies to choose from during learning activities'. Teaching and Learning Toolkit.

Get better by going meta!

Case study – GCSE PE

It's useful to think about how your *own* mindset and your ways of developing better metacognition and self-regulation strategies can help raise your pupils' achievement. (Bear in mind that pupils don't always like being made to think and that it's time-consuming to build in activities that promote thought and reflection.)

The following extended example of an underachieving and disaffected class shows how one teacher used metacognitive and self-regulation strategies to raise achievement:

CASE STUDY

Phil was frustrated with his GCSE PE class. They had picked the subject because they enjoyed the practical side, but they made little effort with learning the complex, scientific terminology needed to succeed in the examination.

Understanding that metacognitive strategies might help, Phil set out to get his class to think explicitly about their learning processes. He held a frank discussion with them about what they were finding challenging about the course. He realised that although they were clear about what they needed to do to be successful in sport, they weren't as clear about or engaged with the examination requirements. He decided to tackle this.

Case study – GCSE PE

Talking about their own learning

Metacognition demands understanding and
involvement from pupils.

CASE STUDY

Phil's students were unclear about the assessment criteria they
needed to address for the year. He made a list of the key skills
and areas that they would be assessed on and discussed these
with them.

Then they privately self- assessed their own competence in these
areas, awarding themselves a red/ amber/ green rating according
to their perceived strengths. This gave him a useful insight into
their views and attitudes: sometimes they imagined weaknesses
that didn't exist and other times they overestimated their skills.
They then discussed what they found particularly challenging
about learning for the examination. This highlighted some
particular concerns such as how to learn complex scientific
vocabulary and how to write more extended answers.

Case study – GCSE PE

Be flexible and match strategy to problem

It's important to adapt your teaching techniques to the class in question.

Phil's class felt insecure in their learning and didn't like being put on the spot as individuals, so he organised them into teams of three. He also tapped into their love of practical skills, to make the difficult learning and retention of technical terms a challenging 'game'.

In the corner of the room Phil posted a large copy of a complicated diagram of the circulatory system. In their teams, students were numbered 1-3. All the number 1's had to go and study the diagram, return to the group and explain it to the number 2, who drew it, while number 3 now went to study the original diagram. The group's aim was to remember and replicate the diagram with accurate labelling, spelling and scale. Everybody was engaged and Phil's students were amazed by how much they recalled and how much they enjoyed learning complex information.

By understanding the barriers to pupils' learning, Phil was able to adapt his lesson to develop their confidence and help them start on the pathway to success.

Case study – GCSE PE

Get talking together for co-constructed success criteria

Sharing with the class what you are looking for in their work demystifies the assessment process and helps them succeed. This means ensuring that the learning objectives (LO's) and success criteria (SC) are both clear, specific and straightforward to understand.

CASE STUDY

Phil made clear what he expected from his class; however he knew that their learning was really cemented when they were able to co-construct success criteria with him. Together they discussed in class what would be reasonable for them to achieve and how it related specifically to the success criteria for each particular task.

Being involved in setting the success criteria and understanding the rationale behind what they were doing, had a beneficial **meta side effect**: students became much more motivated about their learning.

Case study – GCSE PE

Why LO's and SC matter

Multiple research indicates that sharing and co-constructing success criteria is highly effective in raising results for pupils of all ages. When you know exactly what you're aiming for and how you will be judged, motivation soars. Students gain confidence and control over their learning.

Phil found that although his class could explain the criteria for success – they didn't always know what success looked like. Showing them examples and getting them to discuss which criteria they demonstrated made it more explicit and helped them achieve top quality results.

Key meta questions in every lesson:
- *What are we learning today?*
- *How will we know when we have been successful?*
- *What will help us succeed in this task?*
- *What should the success criteria be for this task?*
- *How well have you met the success criteria?*

Indications of metacognition and self-regulation in the classroom

When pupils are used to thinking about their learning and acting on this knowledge there are clear signs of engagement, reflective thought and progress within the classroom.

Ross, Year 9, shows metacognitive skills in his everyday approach to lessons:

- I can review my work and I know how to improve
- Mistakes are only temporary! I'll learn from that error next time
- *Sir, you explained 'mode' really well, but I am confused by the chart. Can you explain why..?*
- I know how to find this out for myself! I'll double check my workings
- I understand the success criteria and have checked my work against it
- I know the most effective way to revise for tests

Testing Times

Revision

In schools, achievement is usually ultimately measured by examination and test results. Accordingly, students have to be confident about tackling these assessments in ways that allow them to demonstrate what they know, understand and can do.

Great teachers make revision lessons useful, engaging and memorable – and, crucially, they don't leave it all to the last minute! They build in plenty of active reflection time so that pupils are always expanding and consolidating their knowledge well ahead of the test date.

This section of the Pocketbook looks at what makes effective revision. It includes some interactive, stimulating and memorable teaching techniques that will equip pupils with the knowledge and self-reflective skills to succeed in exams. It's about empowering them to remember what they've learnt and to be able to apply it in test situations.

We'll look first at six principles for test-taking success, then at some interactive lesson ideas that can make all topics engaging and memorable.

Six principles for test-taking success

1. Teach backwards

True story – strategic revision

David, a bright college medical student, expected to do well in his end of term exam. He knew the topics inside out. However, when he got his results he'd narrowly failed. Despite knowing his subject well, he wasn't briefed on how he'd be assessed. He was unfamiliar with the mark scheme and what he needed to show to get full marks. David hadn't revised strategically enough. After a thorough study of the exam requirements, he retook the paper and earned one of the top marks in his year.

Top test results depend on more than just good subject knowledge. Teachers who ensure pupils get great scores get strategic: they master 'teaching backwards'. Looking at sample papers, mark schemes and assessment material is a crucial first step in ensuring that students are perfectly prepped for exam success.

- What exactly needs to be covered from the exam specification?
- How much are different components worth?
- Can pupils re-take or re-submit work?
- How long do you have to cover the course, factoring in other school events, and what, therefore, is the best way of using time to give students the best chance of success.

2. Share the criteria

Just as important as mastering teaching backwards is getting your students involved and immersed in the assessment process. Great teachers secure test success by ensuring their pupils are fully conversant with the test requirements. Are they clear about:

* Timings. How much each component is worth
* Number of sections to complete. Percentage of marks each question is worth

As with David earlier, students need to understand the detail behind the test mark scheme and the skills and expertise they need to demonstrate.

* Does the question require them to compare?
* Will they get marks for showing their workings?
* Does writing in sentences matter or are bullet points enough?
* Will they be rewarded for using specialist vocabulary?
* Do they need to give a certain number of examples?

These critical pieces of information can make or break examination performance.

3. Enough (exam) practice makes perfect

'We are training to become examiners!' (**motivated Year 10 pupil.**)

Pupils certainly need plenty of timed examination practice, but a key way to help them develop mastery of a topic is to ask them to create suitable examination style questions with accompanying mark schemes themselves, thereby becoming 'as good as examiners'.

A GCSE Maths teacher who achieves superb results uses this approach. She first of all shares the 'big picture' of what the class will be covering that term but then, rather than just covering the topic, eg trigonometry, and leaving exam practice until later, she ensures the class knows from the start what trigonometry questions are likely to look like in the exam. Her students regularly create suitable exam questions and devise accompanying mark schemes. They 'test' and 'mark' each other on these. This embeds their understanding, helps them see how they will be assessed and cements their learning.

Faced with the 'real' GCSE paper in the exam hall, they know exactly what the examiner is looking for and how to work out from the question what mathematics is being tested.

4. Learn the language of success

Pupils' literacy skills often hold the key to exam success. Most schools have early literacy interventions to boost basic skills, but *all* pupils need to develop the precise subject-specific literacy skills to enable them to tackle exam questions with ease. Take this Science exam question:

> *Aluminium is made by the reduction of molten aluminium ore, using a very large amount of electricity. How is iron ore reduced in a blast furnace to make iron?*

To succeed, pupils need to be able to read accurately, understand the scientific terms and write about them clearly.

Teachers who have boosted pupils' exam results use active reading strategies in class. They also focus on helping their students to learn subject-specific key words and to refine their writing skills for exam purposes. These elements need to be thoroughly embedded throughout the course, rather than taught at the end as part of last minute exam preparation!

For more information on this area see: *Literacy Across the Curriculum Pocketbook*.

5. Track for success – self-reporting

When pupils track their own success – self-reporting and predicting their grades – their achievement rises. Below, a GCSE student uses a skill sheet to show how well she thinks she has mastered key criteria in an assignment. Afterwards, her teacher completes it and discusses her findings with her.

Reading response to *My Last Duchess* by Robert Browning

Skills	Pupil rating (red, amber, green)	Pupil comment	Teacher comment
Secure use of brief quotation	*green*	*I used 6 quotations.*	Several of your quotations are several lines long. To be green make them several words only.
Secure use of poetic techniques	*amber*	*I used various techniques, but I think I could include more examples.*	Agreed. You have confused onomatopoeia and alliteration Check your notes for this and make corrections.
Analysis of quotation	*green*	*I think I discuss the ideas in depth and pick out key words to comment on.*	Agreed.

Pupils who can evaluate their skill progression over time are helped to see what the test or coursework requires as well as to improve their understanding.

6. Make use of marginal gains

The concept of 'aggregation of marginal gains' comes from the successful British Cycling Coach Dave Brailsford at the London Olympics 2012.

Put simply, it's the idea that rather than trying to find one 'magic fix' that will improve performance, there are instead multiple tiny scopes for improvement. Individually these might make only a very slight difference, perhaps 0.5%, but if you can make twenty of these improvements you start creating a very big change.

The same is true for pupils' exam performance – a dropped mark here, a missing question here, a misreading there – it all adds up. Students who maximise their achievement in exams have taken all opportunities to gain the highest number of marks possible.

Like a top cycling coach, a great teacher strives to help her charges take every opportunity to make marginal gains. Just one mark can be the difference between Level 3 and 4, Grade A or B, pass or fail.

Top revision techniques

The best revision techniques tackle pupils' areas of weakness, are memorable, and they secure the learning for that class. The following pages outline five strategies that address the most common barriers to students' learning. Tweak and adapt them to meet your students' learning needs.

Strategy	Useful when
Silent Debate	students are over-reliant on you and not wanting to push themselves
Rapid Exchange of Information	students are not checking and reviewing their work
Quiz, Quiz, Trade	students struggle to retain factual information
Tarsia Puzzle	students don't understand key terms or need practice finding solutions
Circuit Training	students are reluctant to join in or engage with practice tests

Three books which give good revision ideas that can be readily adapted for most subjects and ages are:

* *The Teacher's Toolkit* by Paul Ginnis
* *The Collaborative Learning Pocketbook* by Gael Luzet
* *Cooperative Learning Structures* by Spencer Kagan

Five revision strategies

1. Silent Debate – show what you know

In his book *Evidence Based Teaching* teaching expert Geoff Petty reports, shockingly, that teachers *'often give pupils information twenty times faster than they can process it'*. Effective revision allows time for pupils to think about their learning and to practise and embed what we think we have taught them. 'Silent Debate' is ideal for checking and furthering the learning of complex topics.

At the end of a topic, remind pupils to revise the key areas for the next lesson. Divide the class into groups of four. Give each group a large piece of paper, an exam style essay question (different one per group) and four of the same coloured pens. Without speaking (Silent Debate) each group needs to annotate the sheet with responses to the question. After about ten minutes they take their coloured pens and move to the next table, responding and agreeing or disagreeing with the comments.

Why it engages – The different coloured pens identify which groups are trying hardest.
Why it challenges – Challenging each other's comments extends students' thinking.
How it helps the teacher – You get a clear snapshot of how well each group is doing.

Five revision strategies

2. Rapid Exchange of Information – reflect on your work

When pupils are mid-way through a piece of work, whether it is writing a gripping story opening, planning a design, writing a scientific conclusion, etc. get them away from their tables, sitting in two parallel lines opposite each other with a short piece of their work. Ensure everyone is clear about the success criteria and then ask students to swap their work with their opposite neighbour. They should give two positive comments (identifying what they like about it), and point out one thing that needs to be improved. They quickly feedback, and then one side moves up a seat and the procedure is repeated.

Why it engages – It's fast paced, pupils get to talk to several people with a clear focus and defined outcome.
Why it challenges – Pupils have to think quickly and evaluate each other's work. They can be asked to go back and review their work afterwards, adding improvements.
How it helps the teacher – Students receive precise feedback from their peers.

Five revision strategies

3. Quiz, Quiz, Trade – secure key knowledge

When it's important to help pupils learn key pieces of information, eg when teaching a topic with a number of key terms, definitions or right answers, the following makes a fun plenary activity to check learning.

Give each pupil a question card, eg: 'Who was King Henry VIII's second wife?' Pupils have to walk around the room asking each individual they encounter the question on their card and then answering the question they are asked in turn. If either party does not know the answer, the questioner needs to drop hints to help (answers should be written on back of card). When both have correctly answered their question they 'trade' cards and move on to ask someone else the new question.

Why it engages – Pupils enjoy being 'quizmaster' and can work quickly round the room.
Why it challenges – Students have to give right answers; you can set them a target of how many questions they must answer correctly in, say, three minutes.
Why it helps the teacher – It secures key knowledge and you can see how well pupils are responding.

Five revision strategies

4. Tarsia Puzzle Maker – link key terms

The word 'Tarsia' refers to a form of mosaic decorative art, or the act of creating such a mosaic. Google 'Tarsia' for freely available software and applications that allow you to create various interlinking puzzles, jigsaws, card games etc that connect answers to questions to reinforce learning with students.

You can create Maths Tarsia where answers to questions are on different cards. Pupils must join these together to show the solution. Alternatively, you or your students could make a Tarsia using key terms and definitions in, say, RE. Pupils have to find the phrase that defines 'reincarnation', 'karma' or 'relic' matching the term to the definition.

Why it engages – It's interactive and provides quick bursts of activity related to learning which inspire and interest pupils.
Why it challenges – You can increase the challenge by giving students a limited amount of time to complete their Tarsia.
Why it helps the teacher – It's an engaging way of securing pupils' knowledge of key terms and can be used as a quiz to check learning. It's easy to see how well students are doing.

Five revision strategies

5. Circuit Training – test techniques

Many pupils struggle to get engaged with revision. This motivating idea comes from the real fitness regime where you spend a limited amount of time on a 'station' completing a specific targeted activity such as thirty press ups, before moving into a different station and, say, skipping for five minutes. Circuit training is not just for PE! Set up different tasks with instructions on various tables around the room. Pupils work in pairs, starting at different work stations. In a class of 30, with five stations, three pairs could start at each station. After a given time limit students move on to the next station to tackle the new tasks/ challenges.

Why it works – It's pacy and it allows students the opportunity to discuss.
Why it challenges – You can give students 'circuit sheets' on which to record their answers, with rewards for the best pair. You can colour code different tasks for different challenge levels, perhaps providing pointers on the back of the instructions for pupils who get stuck.
Why it helps the teacher – It gives quick exam practice in an engaging way.

Pupils, Parents
and Partners

Make every opportunity count!

It's important to make lessons as engaging as possible to ensure good quality learning but, of course, pupils are at home much more than they are at school. Parents, carers and other youngsters exert huge influence over individuals' attitudes to learning. Parental involvement that helps pupils have high expectations of themselves is rated as having a 0.49 effect size in John Hattie's research synthesis.

Interestingly, a report by the Sutton Trust highlighted 'no significant difference between high-income and low-income parents in their views about the importance of providing support at home for their children's reading and other school work.' However, working longer hours to earn enough to get by puts pressure on parents' ability to support their children's learning.

Schools that have successfully raised achievement involve others in the learning process. This chapter looks first at how pupils can 'coach' each other to attain better results and then at how schools get families involved in raising achievement.

Peer to peer learning

The research demonstrates that getting students involved in teaching each other is very effective in raising achievement, both for the students doing the teaching and for those being taught by their peers. There are three main ways of implementing this:

1. Using '**peer buddies**' to develop good peer assessment/ review practices in the classroom.

2. **Pupils teaching** the whole class or a group and becoming 'experts' in a particular area.

3. **More expert students coaching/ mentoring less able pupils**. Here the 'experts' enhance the 'know how' and understanding of those less proficient than themselves. This needs carefully handling so that all pupils are learning and securing knowledge – not just teaching others. It's often most successful when the 'coaching' takes place outside of established lessons or when, as in the case of PE, the ability to 'coach' others is part of the assessment criteria for the subject.

Peer learning buddies

'Working with my partner really makes me think about my work. He knows what I need to focus on and it's really useful when we discuss my work and check it against the success criteria.' Mia, Year 5.

One teacher establishes 'peer partners' throughout the year, carefully 'buddying up' pupils with similar levels of ability and complementary skills. Students are used to working cooperatively and offering constructive feedback on each other's work. The class has agreed guidelines for their comments. Pupils have effective discussions about the strengths and weaknesses of each other's work. Their books show that peer assessment has helped them improve. They are now confident at reviewing their work and improving on the teacher's specific targets.

Teaching pupils to peer review

Before any successful peer review can happen the class need to be taught to look at exemplar work, compare it against the pre-set success criteria and shown how to suitably discuss its strengths and weaknesses. Age is no barrier. Key Stage 1 pupils are highly effective at giving critiques provided the process has been modelled to them. It is key to have:

- Clear success criteria so pupils know what they are looking for
- Effective modelling (by the teacher) of how to discuss each other's work
- A supportive classroom climate so feedback is constructive

An inspiring YouTube clip shows the transformative power of peer assessment. Here, Austin, a First Grader (age 6-7) in the US, is given specific constructive advice from his peers about his drafts of a butterfly sketch: *https://www.youtube.com/watch?v=JFHf7jAfJlg*

Over a series of peer feedback sessions, during which clear 'critique protocols' are in operation, Austin is able to refine and improve his sketch. The results are amazing.

Power teaching!

In the US some teachers are involved in 'power teaching' where students take it in turn to facilitate and 'key teach' parts of the lesson. Pupils learn to be confident about questioning and engaging their peers in discussions. Because the power teaching approach uses lively repetitive gestures and catchy phrases to get *all* pupils actively discussing ideas in a focused way, those who are not 'teaching' are also actively participating – there are no passengers!

Take a look on YouTube for examples of 'power teaching' in practice.

In the '11 year old teacher' clip: *www.youtube.com/watch?v=FhvaDFwmfBY* the pupil gets her classmates to discuss a piece of writing: how far is it successful as a written piece? Notice how her peers are fully engaged in the detail of the work and notice the value of the feedback to the observing teacher. He can spot gaps in understanding and note the level of contributions.

Even if you don't fancy this formal way of creating 'pupil power', just making sure pupils get opportunities to teach each other key concepts from time to time is a useful way of helping them to cement their learning.

Pupil mentors

Often pupils who underachieve don't make their needs known or they miss the opportunity to have an important misconception rectified by the teacher. Sixth form pupils make great subject-specific mentors. They can conduct one-to-ones at break or lunchtime, or even provide support within lessons. Students studying at 'A Level' definitely have enough subject knowledge to support younger pupils who are struggling.

One top achieving secondary school advertised for sixth form mentors for Year 9 pupils at risk of underachievement in Maths or English. Volunteers received training from a subject teacher about what to look for in pupils' work, and how to ask questions to encourage pupils to explain what they did not fully understand. Each sixth former mentored two pupils. They met with them weekly looking through their work and helping them to understand.

The sixth form mentors evaluated the project: they found helping pupils to make progress rewarding – and invaluable on their university applications. One had decided to become a teacher! Most importantly, the pupils who had been mentored had significantly increased their test scores and confidence in that subject area.

Mentoring matters!

Many schools are involved in broader mentoring programmes. These can transform attitudes to learning. Often pupils feel having to be publicly accountable to a named member of staff and receiving regular encouragement keeps them on track with their studies. Mentoring can help students improve in a range of situations, eg: developing better organisational skills, keeping up-to-date with homework, being motived to study, etc.

Mentoring can be particularly successful with pupils who are very aware of peer pressure:

> '*Many boys, in particular have achieved far better than predicted on the basis of previous performances, because they have developed a sense of self belief, and come to realise that they can reconcile academic work with the self-image which they wish to promote.*'
>
> (*Raising Boys' Achievement Research*, Brief no RB636, Younger & Warrington)

Having a mentor can give some 'cool' pupils an excuse to be seen to be working hard and succeeding.

Mentoring methods

Good mentoring practice means that:

- Mentoring sessions are carefully scheduled and run regularly
- Pupils are allocated the most appropriate mentor to them – paying attention to personality and skills of all involved
- Mentoring sessions have a clear purpose and clearly defined targets. These are best defined as SMART targets: specific, measurable, achievable, relevant and time-related. The mentor can help the pupil follow up on what they need to do to succeed
- Pupils develop independence and don't over-rely on their mentor
- Recording and monitoring sessions help keep the mentee on track
- Training for mentors is of good quality
- Mentors and class teachers share information about how the pupil is progressing. This keeps the mentoring focused on the right areas

Involve parents and carers

> *'Family Learning is a powerful tool for reaching some of the most disadvantaged in our society. It has the potential to reinforce the role of the family and change attitudes towards education, helping build strong local communities and widening participation in learning.'*
>
> **(DfES, Excellence in Schools p. 53)**

Schools that succeed in raising achievement actively involve parents, carers and the extended family in their children's learning. (I'll be using the term 'parents' to cover all these groups.). Parents need to feel comfortable talking to teachers, raising concerns and asking for help with supporting their child at home.

Where parents have had negative experiences of school as children, it is important to show them that schools today are different; they can get involved and in doing so help their child to achieve.

Family learning

There are numerous events and programmes that schools can use to support the family's view of learning. Tailor them to the needs of your parents and pupils, then evaluate whether they achieved what you hoped and identify what could still be improved. There are broadly four types of approach:

1. **Getting parents involved in helping their children to study** – eg providing resources and equipment to support pupils at home, and running events where parents can find out how to help, support and encourage pupils at home.

2. **Helping parents and carers overcome social, emotional and economic barriers to learning** – eg working with other agencies, providing counselling services and helping parents access external support.

3. **Raising parental expectations** about what pupils can achieve and their future prospects, careers advice and Higher Education opportunities.

4. **Educating parents** – eg running classes and sessions to help improve their skills in say, basic numeracy and literacy, parenting or dealing with teenagers.

Harness parental power

True story

Near exam time a father was observed in Waterstones looking through the revision books for a key subject. He viewed several then said: 'I wish I knew which exam board she was with...'

Not all parents will know how to help their children with their work, nor understand what pupils could be doing to help themselves improve. This is why it's so beneficial to invite parents along to Learning Evenings, short sessions where a subject teacher explains what pupils can do at home to further their study. Resources are demonstrated and pupils and parents together have a go at trialling them. Revision books and helpful websites are shown and advice is given about supporting children with homework – rather than completing it for them! Parents leave knowing what they can do to assist their child's learning.

Some parents are very 'hard to reach' and feel daunted about coming into school. Running events in the local area rather than the actual school can encourage these parents to attend.

Parental support for literacy

A school was working hard to improve pupils' reading skills. Knowing that some pupils did not get many opportunities to read to parents at home, they organised a range of literacy-boosting activities, including parent information evenings with 'advice on hearing your child read', exciting extra-curricular author events with 'real' writers, parent/ pupil reading breakfasts, etc.

Data indicated that middle ability white working class boys were falling behind. Some events were particularly targeted at this group, including an evening about promoting literacy skills where the school hosted a book stall from which pupils could select a free book.

Evaluations showed that parents found these types of events incredibly useful because they got specific advice about activities they could do at home that would improve their child's literacy skills. The reading scores of pupils whose parents became involved improved hugely, as did the children's attitude towards reading.

Bridging events

Good practice

As well as running various essential 'catch up' classes and extra activities in school time for pupils, one school runs a range of additional after-school activities for pupils who have lower than expected levels of literacy and numeracy. Parents are encouraged to join in.

Several times a year they run Year 6 & 7 Family Workshops with a variety of engaging and interesting maths and literacy challenges. These are fun games and activities based on challenges relating to these subjects. Pupils and parents form teams together and compete to solve problems and win rewards connected to learning, such as equipment and reading books.

Evaluations show that parents find these activities useful and a good way of connecting with their children. It helps them understand how they can talk to them about their learning in the real world – and make it fun!

Aspire!

'In the UK pupils from the highest social class groups are three times more likely to enter university than those from the lower social groups.' **(Ofsted)**

Great schools foster high expectations with *all* parents. They challenge the *'college or university isn't for us'* attitude and provide accurate information about funding and careers.

Some of the very brightest pupils are deterred from applying to Oxbridge because of lack of teacher knowledge and a mistaken belief that the top universities are unwelcoming to state school pupils. Schools that arrange visits and take part in university taster days empower students and widen access, ensuring that the most able pupils flourish.

- The Sutton Trust Summer Schools (www.suttontrust.com) run free residential university tasters in a range of subjects for Y12 students from UK state schools. (See also their Pathways programmes to medicine and law.)

- Oxford Pathways Programme (www.pathways.ox.ac.uk) arranges intercollegiate events for Year 10 – 13 along with web forums and other support material

- Villiers Park (www.villierspark.org.uk) is an educational charity that runs residential programmes where bright sixth form students work together on challenging topics

Start aspirations early!

One primary school wanted to establish high educational aspirations in all their children. They designated Friday afternoons as 'university study time' and pupils opted to take a range of stimulating courses (including creative writing, beginners' Latin, pen and ink drawing, learning a new sport, understanding chess, Spanish) taught by interested teachers or parent volunteers. Pupils of different ages studied together for six weeks. After this time they either produced a piece of work or made a performance to show the rest of the school what they had learnt.

The courses challenged pupils and helped them realise that they could develop new skills. Planting ideas like this in young minds allows time for them to grow and flourish.

Puedo hablar español

CPD and Self-Audit

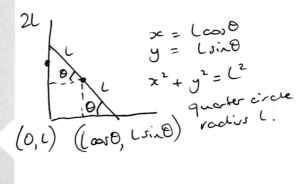

$$x = L\cos\theta$$
$$y = L\sin\theta$$
$$x^2 + y^2 = L^2$$

quarter circle
radius L.

$(0, L)$ $(L\cos\theta, L\sin\theta)$

Why CPD matters

> *A study of the GCSE results for 7,305 pupils in England found that being taught over a two- year course by a high quality teacher adds 0.565 of a GCSE point by subject.*
>
> **H. Slater et al, Oxford Bulletin of Economics and Statistics**

The role of CPD – continuing professional development – in raising pupil achievement cannot be overstated. Research by Viviane Robinson et al highlights the most effective strategy school leaders employed that made an impact on students' learning was promoting and participating in teacher learning and development.

* What sort of CPD have you experienced in the last year?
* How effective was it in improving the achievement of your pupils?
* What evidence do you have for its impact on changing practice?
* How has CPD been tailored to address areas where pupils are underachieving, for example: targeted training on raising achievement for the more able, or strategies to improve feedback, or the use of teaching assistants in the lesson?

What counts as CPD?

Consider a wide range of CPD options and select those that will best help you maximise pupil achievement in the area of most need. These include:

- Professional books and research materials
- 'Lesson Study' and other teacher collaboration projects
- Attending off-site courses
- Mini research projects and learning communities
- Coaching and mentoring
- Online resources and communities – such as Twitter, blogs, websites and Pinterest
- Observing and learning from the best practice

The following pages look at some of these examples of collaborative CPD, while the *Coaching & Reflecting Pocketbook* is a good place to start to find out about reflective practice and how to make coaching work for you.

Books and research materials

There are numerous educational books and resources that can help develop and support aspects of your teaching. (See page 127 for recommended reading for raising achievement.)

Book learning groups

Some schools have set up reading groups whereby a small group of staff who want to improve the same aspect of their performance, eg differentiation or assessment, read the same book, discuss and agree steps forward in their practice based on their study. Schools that work in this way often invest in e-libraries for their staff.

Why not organise your INSET like a **Doughnut Round Reading**. Each member of the group prepares 10 questions they want the group to answer related to what they have read. These might be genuine questions to elicit a better understanding or questions posed to provoke debate and deepen thought. Even better if fresh real doughnuts are involved!

Research matters

When looking to raise achievement you are usually trying to solve a specific problem that someone else has already successfully tackled. Reading research allows you to learn from the hard work of others and to avoid the pitfalls in trying out new ideas.

Useful research organisations include:

- NFER research: National Foundation for Educational Research www.nfer.ac.uk
- CUREE: Centre for the use of Research & Evidence in Education www.curee-paccts.com
- TDTRUST: Teacher Development Trust independent charity www.TDTrust.org
- OECD Education: Organisation for Economic Co-operation and Development www.oecd.org/education/
- The Sutton Trust: www.suttontrust.com
- The Education Endowment Foundation: http://educationendowmentfoundation.org.uk
- Compilation of research by John Hattie found in books such as *Visible Learning for Teachers,* Routledge 2011

Start your own research project

Planning your own research project is an effective way of improving pupil achievement. Creating a 'research learning community' whereby staff bid to receive some time and funding to investigate how to improve the achievement for pupils in a specific group can transform classroom practice and see learning soar.

One school allows staff to submit research proposals. If successful, they are timetabled for an hour's research time every three weeks (essentially a timetabled 'free' lesson). At the end of the year one inset day is given over to the feedback from different research projects. Some of the findings have led to interventions or adoptions that have significantly improved pupils' achievement and excited staff about teaching and learning.

Planning the research process gives you time to investigate, act and evaluate the effect of your actions. Your research can often be used as part of a Master's Degree. By sharing findings across the school, successes and lessons learnt can be disseminated more widely. This way it's not just individual staff developing their professional knowledge and skills; good practice is spread across the school as staff learn from each other.

Using lesson study to improve pupil outcomes

The senior leadership teams' lesson observations in two primary schools identified that pupils weren't making the expected progress. Clear reasons were identified as:

- A lack of challenging questioning
- Poor use of learning objectives
- Inconsistent pupil engagement
- Limited pupil self-reflection

The two SLTs decided to launch an inter-school lesson study to tackle the issue. They first arranged for a high quality external trainer to deliver a bespoke training day outlining good practice, with time allowed for staff to plan a specific area to develop.

Then the SLTs paired up staff across both schools with the intention of using lesson study to develop their practice. It was a significant cost in terms of funding and time but subsequent lesson observations showed strengthened classroom practice and better pupil progress. The following pages explain more about lesson study.

Lesson study – some background

Lesson study is a collaborative professional development process first used by teachers in Japan to observe and critique each other's classroom practice, with the goal of becoming more effective. Teachers around the world are increasingly using it to own and develop their professional practice. Early indications are that it can have a powerful impact on student achievement.

The advantage of lesson study is that it allows teachers to work together in a mutually supportive way on an area that is important to them. The group re-visit and adapt their approaches as the project develops and therefore don't feel under pressure to achieve immediate results. This fits with research findings on effective CPD showing that staff need time, and multiple occasions, to put ideas and improvements into practice.

There are various ways to arrange and organise lesson study. One approach is outlined on the following pages.

Lesson study in practice

1. Clear aims

Teachers, working in a small group, identify a very specific area that their pupils need support with. Alternatively it can be an area of their own practice that they wish to develop. They then consider some specific ways of tackling the issue in a lesson.

2. Select trios

Three is the ideal number for the teacher groupings. All members of the trio need to feel confident and supported by their peers. The trio co-plan a lesson, incorporating the strategies or approaches they think will be effective in addressing the area they have identified. One member of the team teaches the lesson and the others reflect on it through observation of the pupils – focusing on a small group of students works best. Post-lesson the trio evaluate the impact of the new approach or technique, then re-plan, working out how to tweak things before re-teaching the lesson, refined and amended, to a different group.

Lesson study in practice

3. Showing impact
Finally, the group review the impact of the adjustments and improvements, focusing on how far they influenced the learning of that small group of pre-identified pupils. Often these students are interviewed and asked to give their opinions.

Teachers write up their lesson study, recording their progress and findings. In some schools part of the CPD programme is for teachers to share their learning with other staff, either in a presentation or demonstration lesson.

Sometimes the lesson study will have had external input, for instance from an advanced skills teacher, consultant or adviser. This can be useful in providing additional teaching expertise and 'a fresh pair of eyes' but of course any external adviser needs to be skilled in building relationships, otherwise the supportive nature of this approach will be lost.

Planning a CPD approach

CPD helps to improve student outcomes when you cement ideas by using them and reflecting on them. Here is an effective way to think about using CPD to raise achievement:

1. Be clear and specific about what exactly you want to improve.
2. Get clear evidence about why this is an issue. Lesson observations, analysis of test results, pupil voice and feedback are all good starting points.
3. Decide on what specific steps and CPD input you are going to put in place.
4. Research so that you're sure this is the best CPD for you. Will it meet your specific needs? Has it worked with similar cohorts of pupils?
5. Decide what specific steps you are going to take. Write a time-related action plan showing when you are going to do them, and what your success criteria will be.
6. Start! (Be aware that changing habits takes time; you are likely to have some setbacks.)
7. Review. Gain feedback from pupils, their work, observers, your teaching assistant or your colleagues. How can you measure improvement?
8. Reflect! What has worked better than expected, what still needs work? What would you do differently? Are there still gaps that need filling?
9. Share. What successes can you celebrate? Who else might benefit from your ideas? Can good practice be shared within and across your school?

Audit for all teaching staff

An audit is a helpful way of reviewing your approach to raising achievement.
Look at the questions and consider how effectively you are approaching the different aspects involved in raising achievement for your pupils.

1 = Needs attention

2 = Developing

3 = Fully in place

Look at the areas you feel confident about and those that are less developed. These might well be areas to investigate first.

This checklist can also be used by senior management/ leadership teams or by subject leaders to help identify whole school priorities and areas for improvement.

Self-audit

Raising achievement for class teachers	**Current Practice**
1. Do you know the current assessment data for your pupils?	① ② ③
2. Do you know which pupils are at risk of underachievement?	① ② ③
3. Are timed actions planned to address any underachievement?	① ② ③
4. Is there a clear approach for any extra intervention activities?	① ② ③
5. Do you track absences carefully and follow up any issues?	① ② ③
6. Do you monitor the effectiveness of interventions programmes?	① ② ③
7. Do you have regular discussions with teaching assistants and your line manager to review how much progress individual pupils are making?	① ② ③

Self-audit

Raising achievement in lessons	**Current Practice**
1. Do you adapt lesson plans and schemes of work so that they cater for all pupils' abilities?	① ② ③
2. Do you make good use of learning objectives so pupils know what they are learning?	① ② ③
3. Do you use differentiated success criteria so pupils know what they need to do to achieve their target?	① ② ③
4. Are there sufficient resources for all pupils? Can they take them home?	① ② ③
5. Are you aware of the best resources to support pupils at their level?	① ② ③
6. Do you use a range of interactive teaching techniques to help pupils master the subject?	① ② ③
7. Do pupils receive helpful regular feedback/ marking?	① ② ③
8. Do pupils use this feedback/ marking to make corrections and improve their work?	① ② ③
9. Can you see evidence of pupils improving their skills across time? Does their work show that they have acted on teacher/ TA feedback and advice?	① ② ③

Self-audit

Developing your own subject and teaching expertise	**Current Practice**
1. Are you aware of strengths and weaknesses in your teaching?	① ② ③
2. Do you analyse your classes' test scores to identify possible areas to improve in your delivery of key topics?	① ② ③
3. Do you make use of examiners' reports to understand key issues in exam preparation?	① ② ③
4. Do you ask pupils for feedback about the quality of your teaching?	① ② ③
5. Do you share effective resources with other staff?	① ② ③
6. Have you visited another school/ college that does slightly better than your school to focus on identifying good practice?	① ② ③
7. Do you ensure that your own CPD is focused on the areas you need to develop?	① ② ③

Self-audit

Raising achievement beyond the lesson

Current Practice

1. Do pupils have the necessary resources and equipment to study at home? ① ② ③

2. Do you make use of any additional funding for underachieving pupils? Do you monitor the impact of this on pupils' progress? ① ② ③

3. Do you make use of previous students/ inspirational visitors to motivate pupils? ① ② ③

4. Do you use the school reward system to motivate and encourage pupils? ① ② ③

5. Do you ask pupils what else the school could do to help them achieve? ① ② ③

6. Do displays motivate and provide useful subject information for pupils? ① ② ③

7. Do you provide opportunities to engage with parents/ carers about their children's learning? ① ② ③

Finally, make a note of the following:

- What aspect of raising pupil achievement do you think you are succeeding with?

- What further advice, support, training or resources would help you/ your department/ school tackle raising achievement more successfully?

Websites

The Sutton Trust – EEF Teaching and Learning Toolkit
found via www.suttontrust.org.
A useful summary of educational research to raise pupil achievement.

National College for Teaching and Leadership
www.gov.uk/nctl
Case studies of good practice and examples of school to school support.

The Pupil Premium: How schools are spending the funding successfully to maximise achievement
Ref. 130016 11 Feb 2013, available from Ofsted website: www.ofsted.gov.uk

Ofsted
www.ofsted.gov.uk.
Range of useful examples of good practice linked to various themes such as Gifted and Talented Pupils, Literacy across the Curriculum, and Early Years.

Geoff Petty's website
www.geoffpetty.com
Useful insights into teaching and learning, and ways to improve practice.

Websites and blogs

Teachology: **www.teachology-education.co.uk**
Useful cpd training organisation for one day insets and bespoke inset days with a range of top educational trainers.

www.pupilpremiumawards.co.uk
Website detailing information about schools that have won awards for the most effective use of their pupil premium funding.

Teacher Development Trust: **www.tdtrust.org**
A non-profit organisation promoting world-leading approaches to teacher learning.

Blogs

- Mrcollinsreflectivejournal.blog.spot.com (reflective Maths teacher)
- Teachertoolkit.me (general teaching, learning and leadership)
- Ictevangelist – ideas in education especially ICT
- http:/www.geoffbarton.co.uk (ideas for literacy and effective learning)
- Alistair Bryce-Clegg – www.abcdoes.com (ideas for Early Years)